Alan Titchmarsh

LAWNS

HAMLYN

London · New York · Sydney · Toronto

Why have a lawn?

For a start, every garden needs a sitting-place, unle
you're so manic in your weeding and cultivating that y
never have time to relax. Families with children will ne
space for ball-games and bikes, too, so some kind of fi
and reasonably flat surface is a must. This is where t
lawn comes into its own, and even if it's not exactly we
free and not as exactly as flat and green as a billiard ta
it serves its purpose well.

Don't let any expert talk you out of having a law
Although paving, brickwork and other hard surfaces ;
better wearing and less demanding of maintenance th
have one thing in common – they are all expensive.

Only in really confined spaces are lawns more of
nuisance than a pleasure. If your lawn is tricky to mc
and suffers so much traffic that it turns to mud aft
every shower of rain then you should certainly thir
about some kind of paving. Otherwise, relax and enjo
your greensward. One thing is certain. No other surfa
in your garden will show off plants and flowers to su
perfection – even if it is a bit weedy.

Owner's manual

Mow, mow, mow – that's all most lawn owners seem
do. But think about it. Can you imagine how difficult
must be for those grass plants to survive when all th
happens to them, with any regularity, is that they are c
off by their stocking tops every time they grow long
than 2 to 3cm (1in) or so? If you want the best out
your lawn, here's what you should be doing as the ye
goes by:

January – Keep off the grass
February – Brush off any worm casts
March – Start to mow
April – Roll a new lawn if it's lumpy
May – Apply fertilisers and weedkiller
June – Water in dry weather
July – Water in dry weather
August – Apply fertiliser and weedkiller
September – Scarify
October – Spike
November – Sweep up leaves; stop mowing
December – Sweep up any leaves you missed

Mowing

Cutting the grass is essential, not only for appearances' sake and for games of football, but to keep the right kind of grasses growing in the lawn. If you stopped mowing your lawn it would grow very long, but the change wouldn't stop there. The fine, mat-forming grasses would be killed out by taller varieties which were previously unable to withstand such a close clipping. Within a short time the plant life within the lawn would be quite different and quite unsuited to close mowing.

But some gardeners err in the opposite direction. Keep cutting your lawn too close and you'll lay it wide open to suffering from drought and wear and tear. The happy medium is to mow the lawn close enough to keep the hard-wearing grasses present, yet not so close that it becomes baked by sun and battered by feet. Never mow

closer than 2cm ($\frac{3}{4}$in), and in really dry weather, or at t
start of the season, mow down to just 2.5cm (1in). Yo
lawn will still look good and it will last longer, too.

Start mowing in March, and finish in October. Tha
the rule in most years, but if it's really mild before or aft
this period, there's no reason why a growing lav
shouldn't be given a light trim.

Never mow in wet weather. The muddy skid mar
made by the mower will quickly be colonised by mo
and weeds.

The kind of mower you use depends on the kind
lawn you want.

Cylinder mowers Fine, ornamental lawns that dor
need to withstand much hard wear are best cut with
cylinder mower. That's the kind with a large rear roller
small front roller and a cylinder of blades arranged in
helix to cut the grass in a scissor action against a botto
blade. The more blades there are in the cylinder, the fin
will be the cut. This type of mower produces stripes

Rotary mowers Harder-wearing lawns and roug
grass can be cut with rotary mowers. These have a sing
rotating blade which resembles a helicopter rotor. It h
two sharpened edges and spins round at high spee
under a protective shroud. This type of mower must
powered (either by a petrol-driven engine or by ele
tricity), but cylinder mowers may be either motorised
hand propelled.

Hover mowers On banks and over rough ground, t
hover type of mower is very useful. This, too, cuts on t
rotary principle, but it floats on a cushion of air and
glides over lumps and bumps in the terrain. Petro
driven and electrically powered versions are availabl

4

lawn is a perfect foil for bedding plants

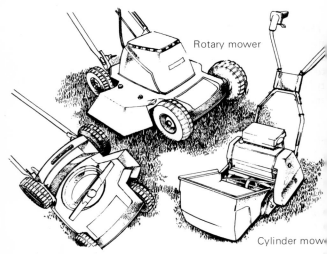

Rotary mower

Cylinder mower

Blade of rotary mower

but the petrol types are often difficult to start.

Before you buy any mower, try to arrange for demonstration. Choose the best tool for the job.

Clippings There's still controversy over whether not the clippings should be left to lie on the lawn or removed. Generally speaking they are best removed simply fit the grassbox to the mower every time you cu In dry weather, though, leaving the clippings on th surface of the lawn is said to slow down the rate of wat loss from the soil. Provided you mow regularly so that th clippings are quite short, there's no reason why yo shouldn't leave them on a fairly rough lawn every tin you mow, but you'd be well advised to scarify the law (see page 8) in June and September to clear it of 'thatch

The grass clippings form a large part of the average compost heap, but mix them with other garden waste to make sure that they rot down well instead of turning to that familiar brown gunge. There's now a compost activator manufactured especially for grass clippings and may be worth a try.

Remember

Mow lightly when the grass starts to grow in spring
Mow once or twice a week in summer
Let the grass grow a little longer in dry weather and leave the clippings on
Ease off mowing in November
Oil and service the mower before storing it in a dry place at the end of the season
Have repairs made at the *end* of the season, *not* the beginning. The queue will be shorter

General lawn care

Edging

If you really want your lawn to show off the other plants in your garden it's essential that the edges are kept neat and tidy. I happen to enjoy going round with a pair of edging shears, but if you don't then you'll have to find other ways of keeping neat margins on your lawn.

Bricks look smart. Lay them on their edges, flush with the surface of the lawn, between grass and border. That way you can mow right over them and save yourself the bother of snipping off the loose ends. Logs can be secured

Edging a lawn with a half moon iron

vertically to create a more rustic lawn edge, but these are difficult to mow close to and a nylon cord trimmer will be needed to chop off untidy long grass.

If you're happy edging, keep your soil edges vertical by slicing them with a half-moon iron once a year. Hold the tool against a sturdy plank if the edge is straight, or against a hosepipe if you're aiming for a smooth curve.

There's a proper way of operating edging shears. Work from right to left and keep your left arm still. Only the right arm should move to open and close the upper blade against the lower. You'll move faster and create a more even cut as a result. You really ought to cut your edges every time you cut the lawn. Sorry!

Scarifying

It sounds terribly severe, and for best results it should be severe. What you need is one of those fan-shaped wire toothed rakes. The idea is to vigorously comb your lawn to get rid of dead grass, known to the groundsman as 'thatch'.

If you don't scarify your lawn, the chances are that a thick mattress of dead straw will build up at ground evel, inhibiting the growth of the living grass and preventing welcome showers from reaching the earth in summer.

Scarify your lawn at least once a year, in September, pulling out all the rubbish and consigning it to the compost heap. Your lawn will look a little bare immediately afterwards, but it will grow away well once it's got over the shock.

If you lack the energy necessary for this vigorous combing operation, invest in a powered lawn raker that's fitted with a grassbox. It does a superb job in next to no time.

Spiking

A whole year of deckchairs, dogs and ball games will leave your lawn with a surface that rivals concrete for hardness. Surface compaction doesn't suit most grasses –

Right: Aerating a lawn; this tool takes out tiny cores of turf. *Below*: Use a wire-toothed rake to scarify the lawn

it makes for poor drainage and a lack of oxygen around the roots. Relieve the situation by spiking the surface of your lawn with a garden fork in September or October once you've scarified the area. Drive it in at 15-cm (6-in) intervals to a depth of 10cm (4in) or so. Wiggle it around in a circular motion and you'll see the earth beginning to lift.

If your lawn is large either spread the operation over a few days, or hire a piece of powered machinery to do the job. Some machines even remove cores of soil. You'll have to sweep these up when the job's completed.

Feeding

Don't be mean to your lawn. Give it at least one square meal a year and preferably two. Proprietary lawn fertilisers are excellent and can be applied once in spring – May is a good time – and again in late summer – August will do. If you can't stand the sight of weeds in a lawn (

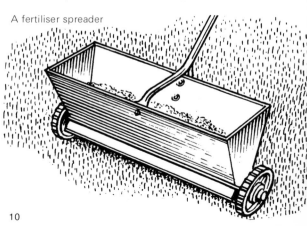

A fertiliser spreader

on't worry too much provided the surface looks green)
uy a lawn fertiliser with a weedkiller mixed in with it.

For goodness sake apply these mixtures with care —
hinly rather than thickly. Put on too much of the stuff
nd your lawn will turn brown, not green. Make sure
hat you water the powder in if there's no rain within 24
ours.

Wheeled fertiliser distributors make even application
asy, and some garden centres will loan or hire them to
ou when you buy lawn fertiliser.

Give your lawn a quick perk up by applying a liquid
lawn reviver at any time between April and August
Sulphate of ammonia sprinkled *very thinly* at the rate of
a clenched fistful to a square metre (or yard) will also
encourage rapid greening. Water it in if there's no rain
within 24 hours.

Watering

rass roots are shallow and so lawns are the first things to
uffer in drought. Don't wait until they are looking weak
nd wilted. Turn on a lawn sprinkler before the situation
ecomes severe. Leave it running for two hours in one
pot before moving it elsewhere.

Rotary sprinklers will soak a circular area; oscillating
prinklers will cover a square or rectangular area and are
djustable as far as direction of throw is concerned.
hey're the best buy.

Rolling

on't do it. At least, not unless your lawn is new and in
eed of a little consolidation. Most lawns receive all the
lattening they need from feet and mowers. Newly

created lawns can be rolled during their first spring if necessary, but use a light roller, not something that's more suited to laying tarmacadam.

Below: Water grass during dry spells, especially if the lawn is new. *Opposite*: Sweep off leaves and worm casts with a besom broom

Leaf sweeping

Grass only grows in full light. Leaves that collect in great masses on the surface will kill the grass. Sweep them off as soon as possible. They'll stack to make soil-enriching leafmould for the beds and borders in the garden.

A wire-toothed rake gets leaves off the grass quicker than a broom, but the old type of witch's broom, or besom, is handy, too.

Topdressing

Real turf enthusiasts will topdress their lawns once a yea
in September or October. The operation is not essentia
but it does pay dividends.

Scatter a mixture of peat and sharp sand on the surfac
of the scarified and spiked lawn and sweep it in with a
old broom or besom. A bucketful of the mixture wi
cover about six square metres (or yards). It work
wonders at improving the condition of the soil aroun
the grass roots.

Levelling

While you're topdressing you might just as well even ou
the hollows and bumps on the lawn. Having first lifte
the turf, fill in the hollows with soil. Firm this into place
then replace and pat back the turf into position. Bump
are stripped of their turf, some soil is removed and th
turf patted back firmly. Small hollows can simply b
filled with fine soil and patted smooth. Grass will soo
colonise them if it's given half a chance, and you ca

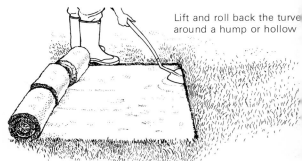

Lift and roll back the turve
around a hump or hollow

Fill any hollows with sifted soil or level any hummocks, then replace the turves and firm

scatter a little grass seed over the surface if you want.

- The idler's way of coping with large hollows is to fill them with soil during April, sow seed on the surface in May and mow in June. By July the patch of soil should be invisible.

'Mow-and-grow' lawn

Lazy bones who want to make a new lawn need buy only a rotary mower. Provided the patch of ground to be turned into turf is level and free of debris, all you need to do is to mow the vegetation regularly.

As the months go by, fine grasses will be encouraged and coarse grasses and many weeds will be killed out. After four or five years the contents of such a lawn will be identical with one which was properly sown. It will never be a bowling green but serves as a play area.

A few helpings of lawn 'weed and feed' will encourage the grasses and discourage the weeds.

New lawns

Apart from the 'Mow-and-grow' method, there's really no easy way out when it comes to making a new lawn; at least, not if you want a decent lawn fairly soon.

New gardens are notorious scrap heaps, and you'll have to clear them of all kinds of builders' rubble and debris before you can make a start on levelling.

Don't make the mistake of thinking that it's easier to lay turf than to sow seed. The ground will need exactly the same preparation for both techniques – grass is grass whether it's growing already or sleeping in the form of a seed. Spread the work over several weeks or even months, but make sure that the following essentials have all been taken care of:

- Dig the ground thoroughly and remove any thick rooted perennial weeds
- Remove tree stumps completely, or your lawn will sink as they rot. You'll be blessed with masses of toadstools, too
- Dig in some peat or other organic matter
- Make the site as level as possible
- Leave the land fallow for a good month more after preparing so that any more weeds can emerge and be controlled

This short list represents an awful lot of hard work, but if your lawn is to last as long as you, then it's as well to do the groundwork properly.

It's up to you to decide on the shape of the lawn, but you'll find that bold, simple lines and gentle curves are easier on the eye as well as the mower.

A fine, level lawn is an asset to any garden

Design your lawn just as you would any other garden feature: lay hosepipes or trails of sand on the ground and view the result from the windows of the house. Fiddle around with the shapes until you're completely satisfied.

Rotavating Some gardeners seem to think that the rotavator is the answer to all their problems. It isn't. If you really want to take what seems like the easy way out you can spray a weedkiller such as glyphosate on the ground where the lawn is to be made, and rotavate several weeks later, but you'll find that:

- The weed roots remain in the soil and may not all be dead
- The ground becomes uneven and very 'fluffy'
- You'll still have to level and firm the site
- Operating a rotavator makes you feel as if your arms are being pulled out of their sockets

Do it if you think it's worth while.

Finally, remember the two main dislikes of grass:
- shade
- badly drained soil

The majority of your lawn should be in full sun, and the ground should be well drained if it's like a bog.

Seed or turf?

Go through these checklists to find out whether turf will suit your needs best, or whether grass seed is preferable:

Seed
- Much cheaper than turf
- Quicker to sow seed than to turf an area
- Slower than turf to establish

- Suitable only for spring and autumn lawn making
- Different seeds are available for different purposes: fine lawns, hard-wearing lawns, lawns for shady areas

Turf
- Much more expensive than seed
- More labour involved in turfing than sowing
- Quick to establish, if cared for properly
- Can be laid all the year round in fair weather
- Available in 'fine' or 'coarse' grades
- Reliable sources of supply may be difficult to locate

Lawns from seed

For a start, choose the right seed mixture for the job. If your lawn is to look like a bowling green and receive no more wear than the legs of a sunlounger can give it, choose a fine seed mixture that contains no ryegrass.

If your lawn is to be rather more hard wearing, but still presentable, choose a mixture containing ryegrass, but look for one with 'Hunter' ryegrass for preference. This type of rye is short and will not produce those long stalks of grass that regularly avoid the mower and stand up like sentries as soon as you've put it away.

If part of your lawn spreads under a tree, seek out a seed mixture that's suitable for sowing in shade.

Preparation   Grass seed is sold by weight. Allow 40g (1½oz) per square metre (or yard) and calculate how much you need on that basis.

With the ground dug over and free of weeds, scatter a handful of general fertiliser (such as blood, bone and fishmeal, or growmore) over each square metre (yard) and lightly rake it in to distribute it evenly.

Now shuffle over the entire area with your feet, rather like a Japanese lady, and rake the soil *lightly* once more. The seedbed should now be level and firm. Too much raking will bring up stones and break down the surface so finely that it cakes in the first shower of rain – so don't overdo it.

You'll gather from this that lawn making is something that must be done when the earth is pleasantly moist, not dust dry or muddy. The two times of year for seed sowing are:

- April and May
- September

It is important to prepare the ground thoroughly before sowing a lawn. After applying a general fertiliser, rake the soil lightly after firming the entire area with your feet

20

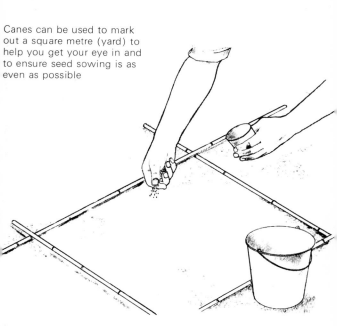

Canes can be used to mark out a square metre (yard) to help you get your eye in and to ensure seed sowing is as even as possible

The September sowing is advantageous because the ground has warmed up, weed growth is less likely, and the lawn has a whole winter and spring ahead of it to become established.

Sow the seed at the rate of 40g (1½oz) per square metre (or yard). This will allow the birds to have a good nibble without the lawn suffering, so don't bother to rig up cotton and milk bottle tops. They won't have any effect after the first few days anyway, and neither will any bird repellent that's been dusted over the seed.

Weigh out the first 40g (1½oz) of seed and tip it into an old cream or yoghurt carton. Mark the side of the container with a felt tip pen and use it as a measure for every square metre (or yard). If you don't know what a square metre (or yard) looks like, mark one out with canes or string before you start.

Sowing and aftercare   Scatter half the seed from the pot in one direction over the square, and the other half in the opposite direction. You're aiming for even coverage.

When the area is sown, *lightly* rake it over to cover some of the seeds. You'll still see plenty of them but don't worry. All you need to do now is make sure the earth doesn't dry out. If it becomes dusty, sparrows will take dust baths in it and that will make the surface uneven as well as disturbing the seed. Turn on a lawn sprinkler in dry spells – you'll help the grass and hinder the birds.

After a few weeks a faint green haze will become visible. When this has turned into slender stalks of grass 5cm (2in) high, lightly roll the lawn (with the back roller of the mower if you don't possess a fully fledged roller), and a day later, mow to cut off the top 1cm (½in) of growth. This encourages the grass to produce sideshoots low down and so spread out to cover the soil. Mow again to remove 1cm (½in) when the grass is, once more, 5cm (2in) high.

Any annual weeds will soon be killed off by mowing. Perennial weeds can be killed by applying a lawn herbicide especially recommended for brand new lawns.

September-sown lawns will need few mowings before the onset of winter. Spring-sown lawns can be progressively mown more frequently, but don't expect them to take too much wear until about July.

Turfing a lawn

First catch your turf. Bad turf is amazingly easy to find. Firms that sell only one kind of turf are to be avoided, even if they do describe their product as 'weed treated'. It will most likely be meadow turf that's been given a quick helping of selective weedkiller.

The best place to locate a good turf supplier is via your local *Yellow Pages*. Enquire as to the quality of the turf and whether or not it is nursery grown – it should be. The firm should offer turf suitable for fine lawns (which will be expensive) and turf suitable for hard wearing lawns which will be slightly cheaper). Avoid 'sea-washed' turf, which is very special but unlikely to enjoy being moved from its maritime location to your inland garden.

Ring around for several quotes before deciding on one that sounds good value for money. If at all possible, consult a friend or neighbour to see if they can recommend a reliable source of supply.

Pat the turves down firmly with the flat of the hand, filling in any gaps with sifted soil as necessary – see page 24

Stand on a board when laying turves and stagger the joints like brickwork

Make sure that the turf can be delivered when you are there to receive it, and when you have a good chance of laying it immediately. It should be stacked grass to grass and soil to soil, or else rolled up. Don't leave it like this for any longer than three days or it will be as yellow as custard and very sick.

Prepare the soil exactly as for sowing seeds: rake in the fertiliser, trample it, and rake again.

Laying turf You're now ready to lay the first turf. Start at one end of the lawn and lay a single row in front of you, patting the turves firmly into contact with the soil. Use your hands or, with care, the back of a spade, but don't turn the turf to mud. Butt the turves as close together as possible, leaving no gaps.

Lay a plank of wood on the top of your first row of turves and stand on it to lay the second row. Lay them so that the joints are staggered, as in brickwork. Work

Chamomile makes an unusual lawn for a small area

forwards like this, right across the lawn, overlapping the edges.

The turves should be of even thickness, but if they're not, it's a simple matter to add or subtract a bit of soil underneath them. A bucketful of fine sifted soil at your side will come in handy for filling any cracks between turves that refuse to sit neatly together.

Aftercare   When the job's done all you have to do is keep people off your instant lawn. Turn on a lawn sprinkler at the first sign of dry weather, or your expensive bowling green will turn rapidly into a collection of shrivelled, brown carpet tiles.

After a month or six weeks the edges of the lawn can be cut neatly with a half-moon iron to their final shape, and the lawn can be carefully mown – not too short mind.

After a couple of months the turfed lawn will be ready to receive a fair amount of wear and tear.

Renovating an old lawn

Here's an action-plan for bringing an old and overgrown lawn back to life in spring. It will take six weeks and a fair amount of elbow grease:

Week 1   Clear away rubble and other obstructions

Week 2   Cut down the grass to 5cm (2in) with a scythe or rotary mower

Week 3   Scarify to remove dead grass

Week 4   Mow down to 2.5cm (1in)

Week 5   Apply a combined lawn fertiliser and weed-killer

Week 6   Mow regularly from now on and treat as a normal lawn.

Chamomile and thyme lawns

Aromatic lawns of chamomile and thyme are lovely things to have, but they do bring their own problems and so are best grown in very small areas – around seats or sundials – where they can be appreciated without driving you to despair. The biggest problem they bring is weeds, for they cannot be treated with selective weed-killers like the normal garden lawn.

If you are thinking of creating a lawn of chamomile or thyme bear these points in mind:

- The ground must be totally weed free before planting (leave it for several months to prove to yourself that nothing lurks below the surface)
- Plant closely – setting the plants 15cm (6in) apart. You'll need about 50 plants for each square metre (or yard)

Creeping thyme

27

- Use creeping thyme or the flowerless form of chamomile known as 'Treneague'
- Water the lawn well in its early stages to ensure rapid establishment
- Plant in April or May for rapid growth
- Hand weed with care at all times
- The first clipping over should be with shears, but the mower can be used later, provided it is set high – at around 6 cm (2½in)

If you can bare to do all this you'll have a lovely fragrant garden carpet.

Problem pages

Too many people worry unnecessarily about their lawns. Unless you're out to achieve perfection it's not the end of the world if your grass contains a few weeds and the odd toadstool, provided it looks good and stays green throughout the year. If you really can't bear a bit of moss or milfoil, here's what you can do to sort it out:

Weeds   Knock them on the head by applying a combined lawn weed and feed during the growing season – that's between April and September. Isolated outbreaks can be treated with 'spot weeders' when they are noticed.

If certain weeds don't appear to be controlled by your 'weed and feed' mixture, I'd learn to live with them if I were you.

Moss   Moss killers will kill the moss that's growing in a lawn, but they won't remove the cause of the attack and, as sure as eggs is eggs, the moss will come back later. If you can't live with moss in your lawn, you'll have to

Weeds and toadstools – see page 30 – are common problems

discover whether it comes as a result of:
- Bad drainage
- High acidity
- Lack of food for the grass
- Shade

Apply a moss killer in spring or autumn, but then deal with the root cause for lasting results.

Toadstools These pop up either from dead tree roots beneath the surface of the soil, or because of fungus diseases within the lawn. They are laborious and difficult to treat with fungicides. Settle for brushing them off with a stiff broom whenever they appear. Autumn is the most likely time for their appearance.

Brown patches The most likely causes are:
- Bitch urine
- Fertiliser scorch

If neither is responsible, look for fungal growth among the grass. If this is found in an isolated area, dig out the patch (well back into clean turf), remove and burn the affected turf, replace it with fresh and water with a lawn fungicide such as Benlate. Scattered outbreaks can be watered with the same solution.

Green slime Slimy green areas are caused by algae. These smelly growths are less likely in well-fed lawns than they are on impoverished and shaded turf. Treat any outbreaks by watering each square metre (or yard) with a mixture of 7g ($\frac{1}{4}$oz) sulphate of iron in 2.25 litres of water.

Moles If you've got 'em, hard luck. You can catch the individuals if traps are laid in their underground runs, or you can poison them with mole fuses (rather unpleasant). If moles are in land surrounding your garden you'll never get rid of them. The local mole catcher or rodent officer should be able to offer you some help, but if all else fails, you'll never be short of finely milled soil for potting compost.

Worms It's necessary to control worms on bowling

greens, for their casts are a prime site for weed and moss infestation. On most garden lawns bowls is played infrequently and worms should be tolerated – they do wonders in maintaining soil fertility. If you're aiming for a fine lawn and can't put up with worms, then water your lawn with chlordane in autumn.

A dribble-bar attachment on a watering can makes the application of selective weedkillers and other chemicals a simple operation

Index